James Monroe Buckley

Two Weeks in the Yosemite and Vicinity

James Monroe Buckley

Two Weeks in the Yosemite and Vicinity

ISBN/EAN: 9783744670593

Printed in Europe, USA, Canada, Australia, Japan

Cover: Foto ©Andreas Hilbeck / pixelio.de

More available books at **www.hansebooks.com**

YOSEMITE AND VICINITY.

By Rev. J. M. BUCKLEY.

TWO ILLUSTRATIONS.

———◄•►———

NEW YORK: ‑

NELSON & PHILLIPS.

CINCINNATI: HITCHCOCK & WALDEN.

TWO WEEKS

IN THE

YOSEMITE AND VICINITY.

Most tourists give but two or three days to the Yosemite; and some, having bad weather, or not recovering from their fatigue before leaving the Valley, are disappointed, and send to their friends and the public partial and contradictory descriptions. Cautioned by old travelers against this blunder, I made arrangements for all the time necessary to visit thoroughly the Big Trees and the Yosemite, and consumed nearly three weeks in what was in experience, and is in recollection, one of the most delightful, healthful, inspiring, and instructive tours of my life. What I saw, and something of what I felt, will be briefly and familiarly, yet accurately, told in the following pages, the friendly letter and not the formal essay being my model.

The excursion was made in May and June, 1871, and we were fairly on the way to the Calaveras Grove of Big Trees when we took the stage for Murphy's Camp, which is only sixteen miles from the Grove. The keepers of the various inns or lodging-places along the route had not been duly informed of the unusual rush of travel, which began about the time we left San Francisco; and at the first stopping place we were met by a party one of whom told us that they had just eaten the last morsel of food in the house. As it was then past noon, and we had taken a very early breakfast, this was painful intelligence ; but, like most bad news, the first account was worse than the truth ; for after some complaint and delay we secured a lunch of bread, potatoes, and pork, which hungry people can dispose of without difficulty, though Jews, Mohammedans, and dyspeptics might find some trouble with the pork. But, as we ate all the landlord had, (as he solemnly declared,) what the three stage-loads behind us, who also dined there, found to satisfy their cravings, we have never been able to guess. We reached the hotel at the Calaveras Grove late in the evening, after more than thirty miles of staging, and to our consternation found the only house full to overflowing ; but after the usual bustle the ladies were accommodated with decent rooms and beds, while the gentlemen were sent into the garret, where there were about twenty single cots. I went to one, and was about to lie down, when the clerk said that it belonged to the hostler ; the next was occupied by a driver, and similar information was given until the fifth was reached, which I was allowed to take. It required, however, much argument, persuasion, and clamor, to get clean linen, the clerk persisting in saying that the bed had not been used ; but a " struck jury " of the guests, after inspecting the same, rendered a verdict that my interest and that of the traveling public required, at least, clean sheets and pillow-cases. Of the twenty men who " garreted " together that night three should never apply to their night's rest the words of the poet, " gentle sleep," for they are sonorous snorers, the unconscious breathings of one in particular resembling a mingling of trumpet blasts and steam whistles, while another's snore sounded like the far-off roll of the ocean. Weary as we were, these " songsters of the night " kept us awake until we became accustomed to the rhythm, which was not until toward morning. After an early and very good breakfast, (for the landlord "knows how to keep a hotel" when he is not over crowded,) we crossed the road and entered the wonderful Grove of which we have heard so much in the few years since it was discovered.

The day was pleasantly spent in exploring the region and measuring some of the trees. You will not expect me to use the marvelous language about the Big Trees which the lecturers and newspaper correspondents have developed into a style as much larger than that of ordinary conversation as the trees are larger than rose bushes. I shall be content with the humbler task of giving you some information taken from accurate sources, and sketching the walks which I took through the Grove.

"The Calaveras Grove of Big Trees," says Prof. Whitney, the geologist, who gives Mr. Hutchings as his authority on this point, "was the first one discovered by white men, and the date was the spring of 1852. The person who first stumbled on these vegetable monsters was Mr. A. T. Dowd, a hunter employed by the Union Water Company to supply the men in their employ with fresh meat while digging a canal to bring water down to Murphy's. According to the accounts, the discoverer found that his story gained so little credence among the workmen that he was obliged to resort to a ruse to get them to the spot where the trees were."

I shall now condense, from Prof. Whitney's work and other sources, an account which will enable those who read this sketch to know without difficulty what to believe and to state about these wonders of the vegetable world. The story of their discovery soon got into the papers of California, and was republished in the "Athenæum" and the "Gardeners' Chronicle" of London. In December, 1853,

Dr. Lindley published a scientific description of the Big Trees, and, supposing them to be an entirely new genus, he named them Wellingtonia, and added, to designate the species, the title Gigantea. But further examination showed that the Big Tree is of the same nature as the Redwood; and the Redwood had formerly been named Sequoia, after an Indian of the Cherokee tribe who invented an alphabet of eighty-six characters for his people. Since a celebrated French botanist, named Decaisne, has conclusively proved that the Redwood and the Big Tree are of the same genus, the Big Tree is commonly called Sequoia Gigantea Decaisne. Prof. Whitney observes that "it is to the happy accident of the generic agreement of the Big Tree with the Redwood that we owe it that we are not now obliged to call the largest and most interesting tree of America after an English military hero." A great demand for seeds of the Big Tree sprang up, and "hundreds of thousands of the trees (millions it is said) are growing in different parts of the world from seeds planted." They grow more than two feet per year; and soon produce cones, which, though symmetrical and pleasing to the eye, are not as large as would be supposed. So many improbable—even incredible—things have been said of the Big Trees, that I was prepared to find them much smaller than they are generally represented to be, but was agreeably surprised, for they are grander and more majestic than I had ever imagined. On entering the Grove a few of the lower Trees only were visible to me, and comparing them with some magnificent Sycamores that stand in an old church-yard near Philadelphia, Pa., the Sequoia seemed somewhat higher than the Sycamores, but not astonishingly high.

Knowing the height of the Sycamores to be less than one

hundred and ten feet, and how easily we are deceived by comparisons of what we see with what we remember, I walked around one of the Trees, and found it as large as four of the Sycamores; and, by retreating from its base to secure a proper angle of vision, saw that it must be more than two hundred and twenty feet in height. I then passed on to examine in rotation all the Trees, of which there are in this Grove over ninety of immense size, besides many smaller, any one of which, standing on the Atlantic coast, would be considered a great curiosity, and would attract visitors from every direction.

The principal Trees have names such as follows:

Name.	Circumference six feet from ground.	Height.
Keystone State	45 feet	325 feet
Mother of the Forest	61 feet (without bark)	315 feet
Daniel Webster	47 feet	307 feet

That you may form a better idea of these heights, I will parallel them with objects with which you are familiar:

	Height.
Trinity Spire, New York	284 feet
Bunker Hill Monument	221 feet

Hence, to represent the height of the Keystone State, we might imagine the Brooklyn pier of the East River Bridge, which, as it now stands, is over one hundred feet high, placed on the apex of Bunker Hill Monument, or a fine elm tree placed as a plume on the top of Trinity Church steeple.

One of the Trees was cut down, and to accomplish it, took five men twenty-two days; and after it was cut through, required three days' labor to make it fall down—its weight being so great that it remained firmly in its place. The stump still exists, having been smoothed off about six feet from the ground, and a small house has been erected over it. I measured its diameter, and found it a little over twenty-four feet. When the bark was on it the entire diameter of the trunk must have been twenty-seven or twenty-eight feet, which gives a circumference of more than eighty feet. It is quite common for large parties to dance on the stump; and sermons have been preached to congregations of from fifty to seventy-five persons, who had abundant room on that singular floor. I was anxious to see the Tree through which it is said that a man can ride two hundred feet or more on horseback; a story which I had often heard but not fully credited. But who shall dispute with facts? There lies the hollow Tree, and people do ride through it on horseback, for which the space is ample; and if it were not, the thickness above for several feet might be cut away without coming to the surface. I also measured several of the Trees and found that the measurements of the Geological Survey are absolutely correct.

The stories about the wonderful age of these Trees are now effectually exploded. Prof. Whitney says, that the rings of annular growth show that one of the largest of them is one thousand three hundred years old. This would be great for the age of a man, and highly respectable for that of a nation; but those who have said that " when Nebuchadnezzar was on his throne, and Solomon built the temple, and Cesar crossed the Rubicon," these Trees were in their glory, have no authority for their statements.

The purity and translucency of the atmosphere add much to the enjoyment of the traveler, as the belt occupied by the Grove is four thousand seven hundred and fifty-nine feet, or more than two-thirds the height of Mount Washington in New Hampshire, above the level of the sea. The longer I wandered through the Grove, the deeper the impression of its grandeur became. Like Niagara, it seems

to grow as we gaze upon it, and the spectacle ennobles all
who behold it.

Subsequently I had the pleasure of exploring the Mariposa Grove, of which I shall not say much for want of
space. It is five thousand five hundred feet above the sea
level, or at an elevation nearly twice as great as that of the
Catskill Mountain House, and is reached on foot or horseback from Clark's Ranch, from which it is about five miles;
over which distance an ascent of one thousand five hundred
feet is spread. Here " there are about one hundred and
twenty-five trees over forty feet in circumference." The
average height of the trees in this Grove is not as great as
that of those in the Calaveras, but the average circumference
is considerably greater. They have been much injured by
fire, yet the effect of the whole, with the Pitch and Sugar
Pines, the Douglas Spruce, the White Fir, the Bastard Cedar
and other trees associated with the Sequoia Gigantea, is
very grand. The trees in this Grove are not named, as in
the Calaveras, but are numbered. I give the height, circumference at ground, and circumference six feet above
the ground, of the five largest, according to the tables of
the State Survey :

	Height	Circumference at ground.	Six feet above ground.
No. 330	——	91 feet 6 inches	——

Prof. Whitney says of this Tree : " Splendid tree ; over
one hundred feet in circumference originally, but much
burned at base."

	Height.	Circumference at ground.	Six feet above ground.
No. 304	260 feet	92 feet 7 inches	—
No. 245	270 feet	81 feet 6 inches	67 feet 2 inches
No. 64	—— feet	82 feet 4 inches	50 feet
No. 60	—— feet	81 feet 6 inches	59 feet

I enjoyed my lonely trip through this Grove, (for I was
on foot and alone,) to a degree which would have reached

ecstasy if there had been two or three congenial spirits with
me.   There are, however, two sorts of persons who might
have spoiled it—the parrot guide, who would have profaned
the sanctity of that " first temple of God " by his mercenary
chatter, and the prosaic traveler, who would have been
continually calculating the number of cords of wood or feet
of lumber in each tree.   I will remark one fact about the
Big Trees, which detracts something from their power to
impress permanently.   Their form is simple and easily remembered.   After they have been once seen, they cannot
be forgotten ; hence, when revisited, they appear just as
they are expected to appear, and the imagination having
but little room to play, the impression diminishes.   It is
not so with mountain scenery, which cannot be remembered
as it is, because of its vastness and variety, of summit and
valley, of gentle slope and precipice, of rivulet and cataract :
nor with the Falls of Niagara, or even of Schaffhausen,
where the rush of the torrent and the ever-changing, never-
ending variety of light and shade defy the recollection and
make it impossible that they should be to the eye a second
time as at first ; nor with such grand works of architecture as
St. Paul's, London, or St. Peter's, Rome, where the structure is immense, and the form, though symmetrical is yet
complicated, and not to be fully comprehended by a glance.
The simplicity and regularity of the structure of the Trees
explain the fact that nearly all travelers are more agreeably impressed with the Grove they visit first.   If that be
the Mariposa, though they afterward explore the Calaveras,
they will speak more enthusiastically of the former, while
the impression on my mind was greater at the Calaveras.
    I will now take leave of the Sequoia Gigantea by ex-
pressing my high admiration of Prof. Whitney's book on
the subject, which was of great use to me at every step,

and on which I relied more and more as I tested its unfailing accuracy. He thus closes his remarks on the Big Tree: " It occurs in great abundance, of all ages and sizes, and there is no reason to suppose that it is now dying out, or that it belongs to a past geological era, any more than the Redwood. The age of the Big Trees is not so great as that assigned by the highest authorities to some of the English Yews. Neither is its height as great by far as that of an Australian species, the Eucalyptus Amygdalina, many of which have, on the authority of Dr. Müller, the eminent Government botanist, been found to measure over four hundred feet. One, indeed, reaches the enormous elevation of four hundred and eighty feet, thus outstripping the tallest Sequoia by one hundred and fifty-five feet. * * * On the whole it may be stated that there is no known tree which approaches the Sequoia in grandeur, thickness and height being both taken into consideration, unless it be the Eucalyptus. The largest Australian tree yet reported is said to be eighty-one feet in circumference at four feet from the ground; this is nearly, but not quite, as large as some of the largest of the Big Trees of California."

We will now take up the journey in the order of time, and leave the Calaveras Grove for the Yosemite Valley. Our route was back to Murphy's Camp, thence to Sonora, thence to Garrote, and thence to Crane's Flat. Very much of the country has been worked for gold, and presents on that account a peculiar aspect. Nature never leaves, after any of its convulsions, the face of a country in a condition at all resembling that of a region which has been worked for gold. Here and there we saw men still at work; and one whom I questioned informed me that his average yield for that season had been about eight dollars per day. In former years, however, the yield had been much greater.

About seven miles before reaching Sonora, some of us left the coach in order to relieve it of a part of the weight, as the hills were becoming very steep.

The Rev. D. A. Goodsell, of Connecticut, participated with me in this pedestrian exploit, and that it may be understood how much the horses were relieved by our departure, the following problem in mental arithmetic is given: If fifteen pounds be deducted from the weight of the writer, and the remainder be multiplied by two, the product will be the weight of his companion; but if twenty-five pounds be added to the weight of both, and the sum be multiplied by five, the result will be one ton. We did not expect to walk more than a few miles, as the hour was high noon, and the sun shone, or rather blazed, upon us most unmercifully; but, through some misunderstanding, the stage passed us, and we were obliged to walk to Sonora, where we expected to find the vehicle and the balance of the load in waiting. In this we were disappointed, as the driver had pushed on. So, after dining in this ancient town, (ancient for California,) we procured a couple of fleet horses, and overtook the party at the next halting place, twelve miles further on.

When we reached Gar-ro-te, a place whose name overthrows the famous quotation from Shakspeare,

> "What's in a name? that which we call a rose
> By any other name would smell as sweet,"

we found the house crowded, and, as three or four loads, averaging fifteen each, arrived with us, where we were to stay the night became a serious question. We found in the party two or three English noblemen, traveling as privately as possible, and more modest, unassuming gentlemen we never met. About ten o'clock the ladies got places to sleep, some of which might be called beds, others were beds "as it were," or "so to speak;" but the gentlemen were obliged to sleep where they could. The English lords slept on the floor in the bar-room; and, though its odors were not balmy, their influence, combined with that of previous fatigue, was soporific. Seven or eight of us were disposed of in a small sitting-room—my pedestrian friend on an antique settee nearly two feet too short for him. I was stretched on an ancient and populous buffalo hide, from which divers fleas were disposed to flee, not further, however, than to the person of the traveler who trespassed on their territory. The rest of the floor was occupied by five men in every possible relation to each other. Daniel O'Connell once confounded an abusive woman by calling her a parallelogram. If he had been of our party, looked at from one point of view, he would have been part of a parallelogram himself; and from another, part of a triangle; and from another, the arc of a circle. But, though neither fleas, nor bad air, nor the hard floors, nor a leather valise for a pillow, could keep me awake, a lusty snorer succeeded in doing so, until, in self-defense, I was obliged to awaken him, after which he could sleep no more, and I obtained a little rest, and but a little, for at two in the morning we were roused with the information that the stage would start in half an hour. Up we sprang and contended for our turn at the tin wash-basin, hurriedly swallowed our breakfast, which was good enough for the price, though we would rather the price had been more, if the quality and variety had improved with it.

At three we left the hotel, all, or nearly all, in good spirits, and about eleven o'clock reached the base of the lofty mountain on the summit of which lies the clearing where the stage route ceased and the horseback riding began. I proposed to one of the Englishmen to walk up the mountain, to which he assented, and we made the five miles in about two hours and a half; traveling at a rate which, though very slow on a plain, any one who attempted to keep with us on such a steep ascent would find to be sufficiently rapid. The superiority of the horse as a traveler does not accompany that animal into high mountain regions. An ordinary pedestrian can ascend a mountain much sooner than a stage or carriage, however light its load, can be drawn up by horses; and a first-rate mountaineer can go much faster than a man on horse or mule back, either up or down a steep mountain road. This statement does not apply to merely hilly roads; on them, in descents and on the intervening levels, the horses make up what they lose in ascending, but it is true of all long and steep ascents and descents. And on any roads, for a month or six weeks, pedestrians can be found who can travel farther and end the journey in better condition than any horses, though the endurance of the mule defies all competition except that of the camel and the dromedary.

Our walk was delightful. The quietness of the wilderness was now and then broken by the startled movements of some small animal or bird, disturbed by our approach, as we turned from the main path to drink at a spring or brook, to survey some immense tree, or to shorten the route by taking a straighter though steeper line, to some distant turn in the road. At each new view of increasing beauty the Englishman would say, " That's a rum view," and if any thing unusual took place he would say, " That's a rum thing." This is an adjective with which the readers of Dickens are somewhat familiar; but if it is to be applied to so many different subjects, its meaning should be expanded by differences of intonation. Our real hope was to reach

the summit in time to make a good selection of horses for
ourselves and friends, but in this we were disappointed by
the extreme democracy of the agent in charge, who allowed
no choice to be made until the whole company should
arrive. So that we had an hour to wait; nevertheless, we
agreed that the walk and subsequent rest were more pleas-
ant than the wearisome lumbering of the stage.

At last all were ready, and then one of the most amusing
scenes you can imagine occurred. Some of the ladies had
not been on horseback for twenty years, and some never.
They were told that to ride on side-saddles is both incon-
venient and dangerous, and that it is much better to ride
like their husbands and brothers. Some of the younger
ladies had an unpleasant consciousness of the novelty of the
situation, and some determined to sacrifice comfort to cus-
tom ; but, after a brief trial, all but two or three rode like
couriers, and, amid much laughter and good spirits, the
cavalcade started for the Valley. My heavy friend, who,
unlike many large men, is well-proportioned and a fine
rider, found a powerful mule, on which he sat with dignity
and ease ; and I procured a graceful and swift pony which
moved under me as easily as a cradle under a sleeping
child. My friend's mule was a remarkable animal. When
all was ready, and the signal was given to start, this mule
looked on his master, looked on the company, looked on the
whole universe as far as he could see it, and opened his
mouth little by little, the mighty chasm yawning until it
seemed like one of the heads of alligators which adorn pri-
mary geographies, and from the abyss came forth a sound
such as only a mule or his father can produce—loud bass,
baritone, tenor, all mixed, not blended, prolonged until the
mountain rang again. It was a trumpet blast, and its inspiring notes stirred every animal in the party. Having

uttered this voice, before my friend had time to deserve such a reproof as Balaam received, the mule straightened his ears and started. We shall hear his voice again.

The cavalcade numbered about sixty, and presented a picturesque appearance as it wound along the narrow bridle path. A more minute description of our route will now be interesting to those who have followed us thus far. At the point where we took the horses, we were some thousands of feet higher than the level of the Yosemite, and were, by the path, about twenty miles distant from the hotels. Prof. Whitney will explain the necessity of thus ascending and descending so many thousands of feet as follows : " The traveler is obliged to rise from three thousand to three thousand five hundred feet higher than the point which he wishes to reach, namely, the bottom of the Yosemite Valley, which is only four thousand feet above the sea level, while the highest point on the Mariposa trail is seven thousand four hundred feet in elevation, and the summit on the Coulterville and Big Oak Flat side not much less." The reason of this we shall understand better when we draw near the walls of the Valley. Moving as we were, along the side, though very near the summit, of the Sierra, and sometimes passing over it, we caught, every few moments, transient views of magnificent scenery in the distance, but for the greater part of the first ten miles the superb forests which cover the region prevented our seeing any thing else, nor did we much desire any thing more grand than the lofty Cedars and Sugar and Pitch Pines, as well as the majestic Firs, which stand like sentinels on every side.

Having a fleet horse, and but little for him to carry, and being accustomed to mountaineering, I formed the presumptuous and hazardous resolution of getting into the Valley before all the others. Of course, there was no difficulty in passing the ladies and several elderly gentlemen, nor was there any trouble in distancing several fine riders who were miserably mounted; but there were several gentlemen who were well-mounted, and capital riders, and had the same resolution which I had made. The superior strength of my friend's mule overcame all the disadvantages of his weight, and he kept well up with the foremost. One reason for our desire to get in first was, that there are but four or five houses in the Valley, the day was Saturday, there were indications of a storm, and we were told that the hotels were crowded—whence we concluded that somebody would have very poor accommodations. Allowing my pony his own gait, I had passed all save two parties, one of three, the other of five, of which the five were a few hundred yards behind the three. I overtook them at a point where the path for a short distance is very steep, and there turning aside at a rapid canter, I undertook to pass them, when, "horrible to tell," the girth broke, the saddle turned, and I was on the ground, not hurt, but demoralized, and compelled to ask one of my rivals to assist me to adjust the saddle and get under way. The fleetness of my horse, however, enabled me to pass all but two, and by one of these I should certainly have been beaten if he had not met with a similar accident. As it ended, the two of the advance party and myself rode in side by side.

There is a partial view of the Valley at a point called the "Stand Point of Silence." I did not pause there, as it seemed better to reach the end of the journey as soon as possible, especially as the upper part of the Valley is not visible at this point. Just beyond we began rapidly to descend into the Valley. It is about this part of the route that such thrilling adventures are told—such as this—" that the overhanging rocks project so that one is obliged to ride on the extreme edge to avoid being knocked off the precipice, which happening, the unfortunate man would fall perpendicularly some thousands of feet." There are, indeed, many appalling depths, and the path is sometimes narrow, and if a horse were blind, and his rider intoxicated or asleep, the animal might wander out of the path and meet with disaster; but there are no places along either of the main routes where one is in danger of being knocked off as stated. There are few points where a horseman meeting another would not find room to pass; and there is no spot where, if horse and rider fell over the precipice from the path, they would fall perpendicularly two hundred feet, though there would be ample scope for them to dash and roll below for a long distance. Any woman not more than seventy years old, if in fair health, can ride the whole distance without any occasion for fright. A very heavy person in some of the steepest descents might do well to dismount, though it is not necessary. Indignation at those who have exaggerated the perils of the route, and thus deterred timid persons from entering, was freely expressed by many; and one of the party of three, an eloquent Presbyterian clergyman of San Francisco, made the whole descent with his hands in his pockets, sitting bolt upright on his horse's back. Both the Mariposa route and that which we took are every way as safe as ordinary mountain trails. Still, let no one expect to find them like the Boulevards, or the avenues in Central Park.

The last five miles are through the Valley, of which we could see nothing, as it was now quite dark. I selected the middle of the three hotels, Black's, and obtained quarters for the eight who were immediately of our party, and while sitting in the porch saw a company of men bringing up the steps what seemed to be the body of a man. On inquiry I found that an Italian gentleman had fallen, that afternoon, over a precipice, and was fatally injured. The poor man died that night. How he met with the accident will be described in the narrative of our visit to the same spot. Fearing lest our party, hearing of this accident, should suppose some of their own friends to be injured, I rode back toward them, and soon met Mr. Goodsell, to whom I communicated the sad intelligence of the accident and the joyful news that we had good accommodations. He informed me that one of our party was badly hurt, not by falling or being thrown, but by a kick from a vicious horse. His wound, though painful, and sufficient to keep him in bed for a few hours, and to excite the sympathy of his friends, was not as bad as it would have been if it had been worse; and by all but the sufferer, and perhaps by him now, may be classed among the interesting adventures of the trip. When my friend left his faithful mule, the animal, with every appearance of affection, turned his face toward his late rider, and made the valley ring again with his mighty voice. The note had something marvelous in it; and to this day we almost fancy that we hear it reverberating among the hills. Some of the ladies, on dismounting, found that their limbs refused to obey, and their mode of motion resembled that of a crab; but the stiffness soon passed away, all had excellent appetites, all were cheerful, and all slept well. I ought to say, however, that the intelligence of the fatal accident referred to threw a tinge of gloom over the whole company.

The next day was Sunday, and it rained from morning till night. In the evening we had a brief service, at which most of the guests were present. On Monday the storm continued for the greater part of the day, and I employed the intervals in riding on horseback through the Valley and making myself familiar with its topography. It is easy to see why we must ascend several thousand feet above the Valley in order to get into it. It is so deep, and has such steep sides, that it cannot be entered from below, but must be approached from above and on the side. (Since my visit, however, the Indian trail, more than two thousand feet lower, has been worked, and I learn has already been, or soon will be, declared open and safe. All robust and leisurely travelers will, however, do well to take one of the high trails in entering or departing, as the scenery more than compensates for the increased labor. One great advantage of the lower trail will be the possibility of entering and leaving the Valley much earlier and later in the season, as the snow will melt in the Spring sooner and will not fall until later in the Autumn on the lower route than on the summit of the Sierra, over which the old Mariposa and Big Oak trails run.)

I am going to give you simply an outline at first, and then describe the excursions made. The Geological Survey, already quoted, says, "The Valley proper consists of three parts. First, the bottom. This is a nearly level area, having a gentle slope. The width of the space between the *débris* slopes is very variable. In the upper part of the Valley it averages something less than half a mile. A little below the Three Brothers it closes to an eighth of a mile in width, and between El Capitan and Cathedral Rock the Valley is narrowed down so that there is only just room for the river to pass. Below this it opens out again, and forms two charming little patches of meadow of about twenty acres each in extent. There are altogether one thousand one hundred and forty-one acres of land in the Valley proper, of which seven hundred and forty-five are meadow and the remainder a sandy soil. The elevation of the bottom of the Valley above the sea level is in round numbers four thousand feet. Through the Valley flows the Merced River, about seventy feet in width."

The walls of this narrow Valley are from three to four thousand feet in height. These are differently named, according to their shape and the fancy of those who have named them; and it is but simple truth to say, that " every portion of the Yosemite wall is sublime." Over these " precipitous, black, jagged rocks, forever shattered, and the same forever," the grandest waterfalls and cataracts in the world dash and foam. If we suppose ourselves in the lower part of the Valley, on the left is El Capitan, " an immense block of granite projecting squarely out into the Valley, and presenting an almost vertical sharp edge three thousand three hundred feet in elevation." It can be seen in clear weather fifty or sixty miles. Opposite is the Bridal Veil Fall, which leaps at first six hundred and thirty feet in the clear, and then plunges down in cascades three hundred feet more. Opposite to this is the Virgin Tears' Fall, more than one thousand feet high. Then, beyond the Bridal Veil Fall, is the Cathedral Rock, whose summit is two thousand six hundred and sixty feet above the Valley. Beyond this, and standing on the walls of the Valley, are the Spires, " isolated columns of granite, at least five hundred feet high." On the other side are the Three Brothers, which rise one behind another, the highest being three thousand eight hundred and thirty feet in elevation. Opposite to these is the Sentinel Rock, which towers above the river three thousand and forty-three feet.

About two miles above the Yosemite Falls the Valley divides into three narrower chasms or cañons; the Merced River runs through the Middle, the Tenayo Fork through the left, and the South Fork through the right. On the left, above the division, rises the North Dome, three thousand five hundred and sixty-eight feet above the Valley, and nearly opposite to it is the Half Dome or South Dome, which is four thousand seven hundred and thirty-seven feet high, absolutely perpendicular for more than two thousand feet from the summit, "being probably the only one of all the prominent points about the Yosemite which never has been, and never will be, trodden by human foot." Up this north-westerly cañon is Mirror Lake, and above it is Mount Watkins. To form a proper idea of the purity of the atmosphere it must be remembered that four thousand feet must be added to the above heights, as the Valley itself is at that elevation above the level of the sea.

Following the Merced we soon approach the Vernal Fall, which is about four hundred feet in height; beyond which, for about a mile, the river plunges over a series of escarpments, forming many cascades and rapids, and then the Nevada Fall is reached, which is nearly six hundred feet in perpendicular height. Behind and above it is the Cap of Liberty, a solid mass of granite, some two thousand feet from its base, and nearly perpendicular. Above and beyond the Nevada Fall are the high Sierras.

By reference to this outline you can follow me without difficulty. On Monday I first rode down to the Bridal Veil Fall, and fastening the horse to a tree, undertook to climb to its summit. A gentleman, just descending, said that he had gone as far as he dared alone, and would return if I would accompany him. After toiling about two hours we found it impossible to proceed further, and at a height of one thousand five hundred feet above the Merced River we surveyed the Valley. At our left, and very close, was the Bridal Veil Fall; beneath was the Merced, plunging

tumultuously along; opposite was the Virgin Tears' Fall, a
hundred feet higher than the Staubbach of Switzerland, and
in all respects more beautiful; just above was the massive,
smooth, white face of El Capitan, now partly covered with
snow and partly hidden by the clouds and vapors which
overhung and almost enveloped it.   The grandeur of the
spectacle defies description.   Descending, I rode back to
the hotel, and thence to the foot of the Yosemite Falls.
These I saw by daylight, and starlight, and moonlight, and
by the light of an immense fire of brush made beneath
them.   How shall I describe them?   All the descriptions
I had read or heard seemed contemptible as I stood there.
A lady from New England, whom I did not know, stood
entranced with the beauty and grandeur of the scene.   At
last, turning to the lady who accompanied her, she said,
"That is kind of pretty, isn't it!"   I felt unspeakable con-
tempt for one who would dare to apply any thing less than
sublime to such a spectacle: but if I were to try to describe
it, and were to employ the most expressive language which
could be commanded, and you were to visit the Valley, and
take my description with you and read it there, your con-
tempt for me would be as great as that which I felt for her.
There is very little talking there.   The common expressions
of wonder, surprise, admiration, or pleasure, are not often
heard.   Men and women gaze and are silent, and even little children are made quiet by the overwhelming majesty
of the place.

On Tuesday morning I tried to find some one who
desired to ascend the more difficult cañons on foot, but
met with no success; all of my friends desired to leave
the next morning, and must ride to save time.   Just as I
was determining to employ a guide, and go with no other
company, one of our party said, "There is a Scotch gen-

tleman in the office whom you ought to see. He says he has been here three weeks, and has walked through the whole region, and if he could find a companion whose wind and limbs were good he would stay a week longer." I hastened in and was introduced. The Scotchman critically surveyed me and said, " How long can you walk ? " I did not like his tone. It implied doubt of my pedestrianism. As I had walked through most of the mountain regions of our own country, and over his native Highlands, I replied, " Eighteen hours without food or drink." He rose instantly and said, " We will ascend the North Dome to-day." The rain in the Valley had been snow on the mountains, and I had not walked much since the preceding summer; but there was no room to hesitate. Though it was more than twenty miles, some of it of terrible climbing, I could not show the white feather.

At eight we started, crossed the Valley, and just beyond the Yosemite Falls entered the Indian Cañon. For a little while we talked; but when the climbing grew difficult we needed all our breath, and hours passed away in silence. No proposition of rest was made by my companion; I would not first cry " Hold! enough." At last, after about four hours, we met a noted photographer, accompanied by his assistant. They told us that the summit was covered with snow, and enveloped in vapors, and advised us to turn back; but that would not do, for neither of us could in honor propose it. On we went, waded through the snow, and reached a point nearly a thousand feet higher than the North Dome and a mile to the north of it. But from that point to our destination we walked on a magnificent granite causeway, sometimes hundreds of yards with scarce a seam. At three o'clock we were on the Dome; beneath were the Tenayo Fork and Mirror Lake; opposite, seeming near enough to touch, the stupendous Half Dome; to the east, the Sentinel Dome, and beyond, the Sentinel Rock, while in different directions we saw the various groups of the high Sierras, from ten to fourteen thousand feet above the level of the sea.   It was piercingly cold, the summit was at intervals enveloped in clouds, and the wind blew violently.   Heaping together quantities of decayed wood, we built a great fire, to warm our hands and show our friends at the hotel that we were really there.   While gathering wood we found a bottle containing the names of a party of four, one of whom was a woman, who had made the ascent some years before.   After washing our sandwiches down our dry throats with some snow water, we began the descent, and though it was long after dark when we reached the hotel, we were in fine spirits and had settled two things, which in our remaining trips received confirmation—one was that my Scotch friend was much more expert in keeping and finding a trail than I, and the other that my eyes were more reliable for distant observations than his.   This enabled each to respect himself, and compelled him to respect the other.   As for powers of endurance, he seemed satisfied, for he observed that "he did not have to hold back on my account."   I did not deem it necessary to tell him that if he had " let out any more " he might have been compelled to " hold back."

The next morning, after requesting our accommodating landlord to keep our rooms for us, as we should not return for some days, we walked to Mirror Lake.   This little lake derives its deserved celebrity from the sublime scenery surrounding it, and which is reflected from its placid bosom; and as the scenery is grander than that which surrounds other lakes, the reflection is more beautiful.   My friend, the Scotchman, whose name is Maxwell, said that there were good fish there, and he would catch some. While he did so I slept, hoping to fully recover from the fatigue of the previous day, which for a " breaking in " was rather severe. The fish, when caught and cooked by a man who had a saloon there, were eaten, but they had a very peculiar effect on us both. We became very sick, and concluded that the cook had used two pounds of grease to one pound of fish. Returning, we crossed the Merced River on a log, and began to ascend toward the Vernal Fall. In every direction the scenery was grand, but when we reached the Fall itself we were more than delighted with its beauty. Three times as high as Niagara—its volume, of course, not nearly as great—it was yet the largest we had seen in the Valley. " The rock behind this Fall is a perfectly square-cut mass of granite, extending across the cañon," and the " path up its side near the Fall winds around and along a steeply sloping mountain side." " The perpendicular part of the ascent is surmounted by the aid of ladders, which should be replaced by a substantial and well-protected staircase." This was written by Prof. Whitney, and the staircase has since been built, so that now the ascent is as safe as the entrance to a church. It was here that the Italian lost his life. One of the ladders rested on a ledge, perhaps ten feet long and four or five in width. Several ladies and gentlemen were descending, and the unfortunate man, when he reached the ledge just mentioned, turned around to offer his assistance to a lady just coming down. When he thus turned, his back was toward the precipice, and as she declined his aid he bowed and took one step backward, which caused him to lose his balance, and he fell headlong upon the rocks beneath. Though the ladders had rather an unsafe look, no accident had happened there, and while the politeness of the Italian is to be commended, and his fate deplored, his death is to be attributed to carelessness. He had, just before, drank a bottle of wine, and though not grossly intemperate, habitually used wines and stronger liquors. If his head had been quite steady it seems improbable that he would have turned his back on such a precipice and then proceed to act as if he were on a prairie.

As it was now nearly night-fall we hailed with pleasure Snow's Cottage, at the foot of the Nevada Fall. Mrs. Snow is a Vermonter, a woman of shrewdness, activity, and disposed to please travelers. She knows how to cook all the plain dishes, and can furnish from her dairy milk and butter equal to those produced in her native State. We had recovered from the effects of our fish dinner, the walk had given us fine appetites, we ate heartily, soon went to bed, and found that "the sleep of the laboring man is sweet, whether he eat little or much."

At half-past six in the morning we breakfasted, and having provided ourselves with a sandwich, set out on a tour into the higher regions. Our route first was to the summit of the Nevada Fall, up a magnificently romantic path by its side. The top reached, we went out upon a causeway of rocks into the middle of the river, and from a kind of cape or promontory, just above the lip of the Fall, beheld the wondrous panorama. Perpendicularly descending beneath us was the Nevada; then the little spot of green, with Snow's house on it; below, the cascades; then, the Vernal Fall; on the left, the lofty crest of the Sierras; on the right, the Cap of Liberty; and in the distance, portions of the main Valley, with a glimpse of El Capitan. Here one might remain motionless for a day, and never grow weary or desire a change of position. My genial Scotch friend suggested that I ought by all means to ascend the Cap of Liberty, and offered to point out the path; but said that as he had already made the ascent, he would amuse himself below. Accordingly I began the journey up. The only difficulty was the steepness, for the trees were burnt off at the base of the mountain, and for the last fifteen hundred feet of perpendicular ascent it was smooth, bare granite. The stillness and solitude deepened the impression of sublimity; the views continually increased in grandeur and extent; and after an hour and a half of fair work the summit was reached. It is, as the name indicates, a mass of granite shaped like a cap, entirely smooth, but having on it one or two trees whose roots absorb all the earth there is. The scene cannot be described, and cannot be forgotten. If you ever ascend the Cap of Liberty, and remember this brief sketch, you will be grateful to me for not trying to describe the view.* I had not been on the summit more than twenty minutes when my companion appeared, and said that he would point out some objects which could not be identified without a guide. He then proposed to advance to the sharp edge of the cliff, and look at the rainbows playing about the Nevada Fall. He did so, and stretching his body far out over the precipice, requested me to sit down upon his limbs, which done, he enjoyed for a few moments the scene, and then offered to exchange places with me, which was soon accomplished. If he had risen, or had been seized with a convulsion, no cannon ball ever rushed through the air more rapidly than my body would have plunged into the abyss. So long as neither of these happened, there was no danger whatever, and the enjoyment

---

* The artist has tried in the accompanying engraving to impart an idea of the grandeur of the Cap of Liberty and the Nevada Fall. You must expand the picture by supposing nine spires as high as Trinity, in New York, one above another, on the side of the Cap, and more than three Niagaras in height, plunging down the Nevada.

9210   The Cap of Liberty and Nevada Fall.

amply repaid the trouble. The descent was soon made, and the question now arose, where next?

In the distance "Cloud's Rest" towered up more than ten thousand feet above the level of the sea, and about four thousand five hundred above our position. After a little deliberation, about noon we started for that mountain. At our left, now, was the Cap of Liberty, and beyond it the Half Dome, whose aspect is as imposing on this side as on the other, though its form is very different. For a few miles the way was quite level, and the walking easy; there was no bridle path then, as there is now, and we trusted to our eyes. Often, on the various tours thus far, we had heard a peculiar sound, resembling the noise of an immense woodpecker; but as we continued to hear it when we were miles from any tree, my companion insisted that it was the noise of the beating of our own hearts. But as we heard nothing more when standing close to each other than when some distance apart, this theory was given up. What the cause of the sound was we could not determine, nor could any of the old settlers and travelers thereabouts explain, though others claimed to have heard it. At four in the afternoon we reached what we supposed to be the summit, but found that there are three peaks, the highest of which had not been visible at all from any point which we had passed before, and that it was at least half a mile from us. On we went, determined to attain it, and ate our last sandwich on the very crest at five o'clock. We saw, from Cloud's Rest, the Valley itself; Mount Lyell, thirteen thousand feet high; Mount Dana, thirteen thousand two hundred and twenty-seven feet high; Mount Hoffman, Mount Star King, the Obelisk Range, and innumerable peaks and ranges, and could apply to it a remark made by a well-known traveler about another mountain, " Only those who

have been there can tell what a mistake is made by omitting
it." We now descended as rapidly as possible, but it was
after eight o'clock, and quite dark, when we turned the
base of the Cap of Liberty and began the descent of the
rocky and precipitous path down the side of the Nevada
Fall. A descent is always more perilous than an ascent,
if the path be at all steep; to make that descent in dark-
ness was perilous enough to be very exciting. Mr. Maxwell, however, was equal to any professional guide, and I
humbly followed. At nine the lights at Snow's were just being extinguished when we knocked and voices were heard.
Promptly Mr. Snow ushered us in, promptly Mrs. Snow
cooked us a supper, and promptly we ate it, and went at
once to bed, declaring that such a day's work had given us
the appetite and sleeping power of growing boys.

At six A. M. we were up, and at 6.30 were off again,
this time determined to "bring up" somewhere else that
night, or sleep out on the mountains. Having reascended
to the summit of the Nevada Fall, we continued our walk
along the side of the river to the Little Yosemite Valley.
"This is a flat valley, or mountain meadow, about four
miles long and from a half a mile to a mile wide. It is
inclosed between walls from two thousand to three thousand feet high, with numerous projecting buttresses and
angles, topped with dome-shaped masses. The Little Yosemite Valley is a little over six thousand feet above the
sea level, or two thousand above the Yosemite, of which
it is a kind of continuation, being on the same stream,
namely, the main Merced. The views there are beautiful,
unique, and some of them very grotesque. About half-way
up the Valley "a cascade comes sliding down in a clear
sheet over a rounded mass of granite; it was estimated at
one thousand two hundred feet in height." Having spent

some hours here we returned toward the Nevada Fall, in search of a log on which to cross the river. None being found, Mr. Maxwell proposed to wade it, and, removing a portion of his clothing, made the attempt, but soon found that he had miscalculated the depth, and became thoroughly soaked with the coldest water. I preferred to disrobe entirely, and avoid the necessity of climbing in wet clothes. We then began the ascent of Mount Starr King, which rises steeply from the shore of the river. The chaparral, a very stiff, impenetrable growth, obstructed our progress at every step. In addition to the steepness, the labor was as great as that of forcing through hedges, and at the end of two hours we seemed provokingly close to the river. But by two o'clock we were as near the summit as it is possible for human beings to get by climbing. Prof. Whitney says : " Starr King is the steepest cone in the region with the exception of the Half Dome, and is exceedingly smooth, having hardly a break in it; the summit is quite inaccessible, and we have not been able to measure its height." We think that we were within six hundred feet perpendicular of the summit. Having surveyed the marvelous panorama, which stretched from Monte Diablo in the Coast Range, near San Francisco, to Mount Lyell and the Obelisk Range, we descended rapidly toward the Illilouette, or South Fork, along which we wandered for perhaps two miles before finding a place to cross. Mr. Maxwell could cross a log over a chasm five hundred feet deep, and his head would be wholly unmoved; not so with me—though under the encouragement of his example I improved. On this occasion I crawled across a narrow log, where a slip would have been fatal, taking the attitude of boys playing the ancient game of " see-saw." It was now five P. M., and we were a long distance from any human

habitation.   According to Maxwell's judgment we began
to climb almost perpendicularly up the mountain side.
Two hours passed in silence and severe toil, when Mr. M.
cried out, " There is a grisly !"   And so it was.   The immense brute, however, showed no disposition to molest us,
and walked slowly away into a rocky cavern.   Two or
three days before another had been seen by a party of
ladies and gentlemen, whose guide formed them into a
hollow square in front of Sir Bruin ; this gave him no al-
ternative but to advance upon them; the square broke
into as many pieces as there were persons, and the bear
went on his way undisturbed.

At eight o'clock, with our tongues greatly swollen and
hanging out of our mouths with thirst, there having been
neither snow nor water on the last ascent, we reached the
summit.   The sun was just setting and the full moon rising
opposite, and they seemed but a few miles apart.   As they
rose and set behind the vertical summits of mountain
ranges, it seemed as though there was an invisible axis
common to both, and that it was so inclined that one sank
as the other rose.   Never have I beheld any thing more
beautiful in the Alps or any of our American mountains
than the blended rays of the rising moon and setting sun
reflected from the snowy Sierras.

In one of our earlier trips, knowing that the Scotch love
and freely use strong liquors, I asked my companion what
he thought of whisky as a stimulant in case of exhaustion.
He replied that he had traveled through Australia, and
many other regions where hardship and privation were the
rule, and had slept out many a night, and that while he
was not a total abstinence man, he believed that " every
drop of alcohol a man takes on such tours weakens his
nervous and muscular system, and diminishes his power

of endurance." This was an agreeable surprise. Up to this point our only drink had been water, but now we could find no water, and our tongues were swollen and painful. Mr. Maxwell produced a flask, and said, "Shall we drink?" but just then we descried a snowbank, which relieved our immediate necessity. Except the loss of a few drops, necessary to reduce the swelling of the tongue, and a little used on the feet, the flask went back as full as when we started. We now walked rapidly along the crest to the Glacier Peak, as my friend and guide thought we could descend it; but it was freezing cold when we reached the cañon, and the light of the moon gave us no help on that side of the Valley. After some debate we concluded to attempt it, but half an hour's work convinced us of its impracticability at night, though Mr. Maxwell and an Englishman named Cross had descended in the day-time. Across the Valley, far up under the Yosemite Fall, a huge fire was burning, kindled by Mr. Muir, a resident of the Valley, who had an engagement to spend the night there with us, but we had failed to reach it. The temperature was now about five degrees below freezing point, ice formed all around us, and our clothing, wet by the water in the cañon, began to grow stiff. We had no time to lose, and walked at a rapid pace to Peregoy's, arriving there at twenty minutes of one in the morning, having walked and climbed steadily from a little before 7 A. M. to 12.40 A. M. next day, making just the eighteen hours I had foolishly boasted of in the beginning. Peregoy could give us no bed, nor any dry clothes, so we sat over the cook-stove until 5 o'clock, when two guides got up and we slipped into their places and slept till 6.30, when we breakfasted and afterward ascended the Sentinel Dome, subsequently going down the Sentinel Rock Cañon to the hotel, which was reached Saturday afternoon at four o'clock.

If you ask whether we were fatigued, truth requires me to say that after turning away from the Glacier Peak to walk eight miles to Peregoy's, if memory had failed we could still have told by our sensations that we must have been walking; but there was not a moment during the whole week's work when we were not in better physical and mental condition than when we began, excepting short periods of great peril while we were descending Glacier Peak and Sentinel Rock Cañons.

There are some, perhaps, who will say, " I cannot see any pleasure, and I do see criminal recklessness, in such labors and exposures." To all such I thus reply: The labor is sweet to a genuine lover of mountains. He personifies every seemingly inaccessible crag and distant summit, determines to conquer it, and, having done so, feels his mental, moral, and physical systems alike braced for further effort in any department. The exposures to an experienced pedestrian are more apparent than real; and the possibilities of accident do not increase danger, because the knowledge of them leads to greater caution; not, indeed, the trembling caution worse than none, but the care which experience and steadiness of nerve render easy and almost instinctive. To those who " can see no pleasure " in such a tour I commend the following incident: " On one occasion the celebrated Robert Hall having ascended the dome of the Radcliffe Library at Oxford, England, beheld with rapture the vision of surpassing beauty, and turning to a friend exclaimed, " O ! if this earth is so beautiful what must the New Jerusalem be ! " Soon afterward the equally celebrated Andrew Fuller was taken to the same spot. After looking around a moment he scratched his head, and said to the gentleman who was with him, " Have you seen any new definition of justification by faith lately ? "

There are diversities of taste, and if you " can see no pleasure " in such tours, can you not spend your summers at Saratoga, and walk in slippers from spring to spring, and drink the waters, and thus evince beyond dispute your manhood, and descent from those brave men whom we reverently call " our fathers ? '

On Sunday I went over to Hutching's Hotel, and listened to an admirable sermon delivered by Rev. Mr. Perkins, a Congregational minister of Ware, Mass., and in the evening had strength enough left to conduct a service of at least ordinary length at Black's.

The Yosemite is more sublime than any cathedral, and the voices of its many waters more musical than the most magnificent orchestra. Standing in awe before the silent, inaccessible, apparently immutable Half Dome, it is befitting us to say, as Moses said among the mountains of Asia, " Lord, thou hast been our dwelling-place in all generations. Before the mountains were brought forth, or ever thou hadst formed the earth and the world, even from everlasting to everlasting, thou art God."

On the 5th of October, 1863, I stood on the Col de Balme in Switzerland. While the guide was caring for the mules, I ascended an adjacent summit, five hundred feet higher, and met there a British officer, traveling like myself, alone. After a few moments' conversation he said, " Look at Mont Blanc, ' with its myriad bristling crags ; ' see that sunlight intensified a hundred times by the cathedrals of ice from which it is reflected ; behold the Mer de Glacé, does it not resemble that ' sea of glass mingled with fire ?' Could there be any thing on earth more sublime ? " I responded,

"It is grand beyond imagination." "But," said he, "there is something far sublimer than this." "And what is that?" I asked. He replied, "That the God who made all this, and by a word could remand it all to nothingness and night, so loved you and me as to give his only begotten Son to live and die and rise for us, that when this wondrous panorama shall have passed away we shall be with Him forever." This, as nearly as I can recollect it, is the conversation which I had with the eloquent and spiritually minded British officer; and in the Yosemite I remembered it and thought, Yes, that God, the Creator of all that thrills me here, should give his Son to save me, is the sublimest of all possible conceptions. May those who read these words have a true sympathy with Nature in its grand manifestations, which cannot but elevate and refine them, and also a deeper sympathy with the God of Nature, who reveals in Christ what the mountains, and the seas, and the stars, cannot tell—his personal sympathy and love for every one of his earthly children.

www.ingramcontent.com/pod-product-compliance
Lightning Source LLC
Chambersburg PA
CBHW032143080426
42733CB00008B/1177